Police Dogs

by Dawn Bluemel Oldfield

Consultant:
Sergeant Troy Teigen, K-9 Unit
Spokane Police Department
Spokane, Washington

New York, New York

Credits

Cover and Title Page, © KellyNelson/Shutterstock; 4, © Tom Vickers/Splash/ Newscom; 4–5, © Radius Images/Alamy; 6–7, © SAUL LOEB/AFP/Getty Images; 8–9, © Luo Li/Redlink/Corbis; 10–11, © Sandra Mu/Getty Images; 12–13, © John Moore/Getty Images; 14–15, © Caro/Alamy; 16–17, © Camera Press/Redux; 18, © ZUMA Press, Inc./Alamy; 18–19, © Margaret Thomas/The Washington Post/Getty Images; 20–21, © Tom Williams/Roll Call/Getty Images; 22, © Monika Wisniewska/ Shutterstock; 23TL, © B. Christopher/Alamy; 23TC, © bikeriderlondon/Shutterstock; 23TR, © Getty Images; 23BL, © John Roman Images/Shutterstock; 23BR, © Tom Vickers/Splash/Newscom.

Publisher: Kenn Goin
Senior Editor: Joyce Tavolacci
Creative Director: Spencer Brinker
Design: Debrah Kaiser
Photo Researcher: Picture Perfect Professionals, LLC

Library of Congress Cataloging-in-Publication Data

Bluemel Oldfield, Dawn.
  Police dogs / by Dawn Bluemel Oldfield.
    pages cm. — (Bow-wow! Dog helpers)
  Includes bibliographical references and index.
  ISBN-13: 978-1-62724-120-5 (library binding)
  ISBN-10: 1-62724-120-5 (library binding)
  1. Police dogs—Juvenile literature. I. Title.
  HV8025.B58 2014
  363.2'32—dc23
                                    2013032759

For more information, write to Bearport Publishing Company, Inc., 45 West 21st Street, Suite 3B, New York, New York 10010. Printed in the United States of America.

10 9 8 7 6 5 4 3 2 1

Contents

Meet a Police Dog

I'm a **police dog**.

Police dogs like me fight crime.

Ruff! Ruff!

Police dog

A crime is something a person does that is against the law.

Police dogs have important jobs.

We work with police officers to keep people safe.

A police dog's human partner is called a handler.

Police dogs help their partners in many ways.

We chase after and catch **criminals**.

Police dogs are faster than people. Some police dogs can run more than 30 miles per hour (48 kph)!

Some police dogs find missing people.

They use their powerful noses to sniff them out.

A dog's sense of smell is 10,000 times better than a person's.

Other police dogs use their noses to search for bombs.

When one is found, the dog sits down.

This tells the handler that a bomb is nearby.

Dog sniffing for bombs

After a bomb is found, the police carefully get rid of it. That way it doesn't hurt anyone.

How are police dogs trained?

We go to a special school.

We learn to follow many **commands**.

Puppy in training

14

Two of the commands police dogs learn are "sit" and "stay."

At school, some police dogs learn to find and catch criminals.

Some of us also learn to sniff for bombs.

Police dogs are taught to stay calm around people and loud noises.

After training, police dogs are ready to work!

Like our handlers, we have a **uniform**.

We wear a collar with a police badge on it.

Police dogs have to be smart, brave, and strong.

Police badge

Police dogs are always ready to fight crime.

We **patrol** the streets with our handlers.

Together, we keep towns and cities safe!

Most police dogs live with their handlers.

Police Dog Facts

- Most police dogs are German shepherds, Belgian Malinois, or Labrador retrievers.

- Police dogs are often paired with their human partners when they are puppies.

- A police dog's most important job is to protect its police officer handler.

- Police dogs are trained to smell bombs hidden in boxes, backpacks, and cars.

Glossary

commands (kuh-MANDZ) orders given by people to do something

criminals (KRIM-uh-nuhlz) people who break the law

patrol (puh-TROHL) to guard an area by walking around it

police dog (puh-LEES DAWG) a dog that is trained to work with the police

uniform (YOO-nuh-form) a special set of clothes worn by all the members of a certain group

23

Index

Read More

Albright, Rosie. *Police Dogs (Animal Detectives).* New York: PowerKids Press (2012).

Schuh, Mari. *K-9 Police Dogs (Pebble Plus: Working Dogs).* Mankato, MN: Capstone (2011).

Learn More Online

To learn more about police dogs, visit
www.bearportpublishing.com/Bow-WOW!

About the Author

Dawn Bluemel Oldfield is a freelance writer. She and her husband live in Prosper, Texas. They love animals and share their home with a wonderful cat named Victoria and one terrific dog, a Siberian husky named McKenna.